S.NO	CONTENT	PAGE. NO
1	PARENTING - INTRODUCTION	4
2	PARNTING – IS THIS ROLE FOR MOTHER OR FATHERS?	9
3	ROLE MODELS OF CHILDREN	15
4	LET YOUR CHILDREN SPEAK, YOU LISTEN	21
5	CORRECTING MISTAKES	25
6	MORALS/ VALUES / TRADITIONS	28
7	GADGET ADDICTION	37
8	LET THEM MAKE SOME MISTAKES	43
9	PLAY DATE WITH CHILDREN	47
10	NEVER LEAVE THEM ALONE	53
11	DINNER TOGETHER	58
12	GROWING UP WITH CHILDREN	61
13	FINAL THOUGHTS	64

INTRODUCTION:

Parenting is the process of promoting and supporting the overall development of a child which includes physical, emotional, social, and intellectual development.

Parenting as an Emotional Job:

Parenting undoubtedly is an intensely emotional experience. There is a kind of pious and pure pleasure of cuddling, playing, laughing, and exploring with your children. And at the same moment, there are the challenges— the moments of stress, anger, frustration, patience, or energy to juggle kids, work, household, and your own personal health and wellbeing. . Children need our assistance, not our anger.

But in the end, it is very important to manage our feelings, because how we react in these emotional moments deeply affects our children's overall emotional health. Studies have revealed that when parents react rudely and with high emotional intensity, children's are more likely to get distressed.

So, parenting is surely an emotional job wherein managing strong emotions is surely much easier said than done. But at the end the effort is worth it, as the payoff is huge, for you and your child.

1. PARENTING -A JOURNEY:

Parenting is a journey that starts the day a child is born and continues until the end of the life. Parenting is a responsibility to turn the children into responsible future citizens and thereby molding them into an artist, prime minister, professional or even terrorist. Designing the future of a child is truly an incredible journey. But, do you know when does the parenting start and when does it end? Parenting starts from the day you know that you are going to be a parent and ends the day when you leave the world. Therefore,it is clear that we don't have to stop guiding till a particular phase of our child's life or we should not be involved with the child's activities when hereaches adulthood.

Children go through several phases of life but it's our duty to travel with them in each and every phase, help them to set the right path, guide them whenever necessary and make their life beautiful and blossoming.

These days the sense of parenting has undergone a complete shift. Nowadays, every parent thinks like, "God has made me the parent of a child; and now I had raised him, provided education, helped him to get a good job, arranged him a good looking and good character spouse according to his choice and finally settled his life". So, I am done with my duties. But, instead, the thought

process should be like, "God has showered the blessing on me in the form of a beautiful child and now I have to travel with him from day one of his life till the last day of my life. So if you were involved in the parenting only during his infancy stage and got less involved with their activities in the later adulthood stage then it is definitely not the parenting in the real sense.

Child with parents Earlier, almost all of our parents were financially weaker but psychologically richer than us. Nowadays as we are financially stronger than our parents but we are psychologically poor with stress in our heads at all the times. And to combat it, we need stress busters, relaxation therapies and different distress programs to keep ourselves mentally healthy.

But the question here is do we really need all these relaxation techniques even when we are bestowed with a beautiful gift in the form of the child? If you do the parenting journey very well you will be the wealthiest, healthiest and of course the happiest person in the world both physically and psychologically.

Moving further,another term broadly used nowadays in the process of parenting is "generation gap"? If your child is not listening to you, then there might be some problem with you not with your child. Because you don't keep yourself in pace with your child and are not updating yourself to their level. So the need of the hour is to keep yourself updated till the last day of your life. Don't get disconnected with your children and technology which would make your living worth.

In the end, the conclusion is parenting is an art that one must be proud of and more importantly must be an enjoyable and fulfilling journey and not the burden in any sense. And main focus should be on the concept that parenting in not one day task or one stage task it is a lifelong journey which should been joyable.

Generation Gap – between father and son

2.Parenting- Is this Role for mothers or fathers ?

Role of Fathers in Parenting

It is very important to understand that whose role is parenting. Whether it is a mother's role or the father's role?

Let's analyze a situation before actually getting into the answer. Let's take the example of a rowing boat. A rowing boat can easily be handled by a single person who can drive the boat putting all his efforts in.

And at the same time, it can be handled by two persons as well. Now if both the persons rowing the boat are strangers then it will be a bit difficult as each person will have his own style of riding and so the lack of coordination will matter. As a result, the boat will move but not in the desired direction and speed.

Now consider another situation where the rowing boat is riding by another two persons and both of them are friends. Here the boat will travel very easily in the desired direction and desired speed because both the people have a better coordination and so will work together with a team spirit and will be in the mood of enjoying the nature as well.

The intent of the above example with two different situations is similarly applicable to the process of parenting. No doubt parenting can be done by a single parent either by a father or a mother. But it is a bit difficult to handle the child by a single parent in all the circumstances; sometimes favorable and sometimes unfavorable. Moreover, there will be no partner to discuss before deciding anything regarding the future of the child. So a single parent has to be conscious in taking all the decisions of the child.

Now if the child is raised by both the parents and both will have their own style of parenting. In this situation, the future of the child will be designed in a new route that will not be effective at all.

 In contrary to this if both the parents follow the same style of parenting or coordinate with each other very beautifully the child will obviously reach newer heights because his upbringing will be the result of proper coordination and balancing style of parenting which is strong enough to make the kids strong both physically and psychologically.

In the process of parenting,a significant role is played by a mother in the infancy stage of the child because there is always an emotional connection between the two. And gone are the days, when a father's role was just limited to being a "breadwinner" for the family. Nowadays, his involvement equally affects the child's overall personality and behavior and can be just as loving and nurturing as the mother.

Mothers are not enough to handle the parenting role; both mothers and fathers are equally important in the parenting process and both have to put their hands together and work together with sincerity, effort, and enjoyment to design the future of the child. Therefore, parenting is not dedicated to only the mother but the fatherplays an equal and important role in parenting. But the key is balance in both the techniques of parenting.

Balancing the parenting styles for an effective parenting involves a number of different factors. Few of them includes supporting each other in parenting, getting together in the key values, careful thought, and action, proper communication between the parents, planning the best for their child based on the consent of both the parents etc.

Also, it is recommended not to disagree on parenting in front of the kids. If one of you has to let the other parent take the lead in a given situation, let that happen and then talk about it later.

The conclusion is both the parenting styles are unique in their own ways and equally good for the child. But a blend and a balance of both the parenting styles is really an effective approach in the process of parenting and can be truly amazing and worth all the work.

And if both the parents are unable to coordinate together no one in this world will take care of your child. Because in the end it is your child and so it is you only who matters the most to him!!

3.Role Models of Children

Do you know who the first Superhero of your kid is? Is it Spiderman, Mighty raju or ChotaBheem? But it is no one among the above as the child's first superhero is his parents.

To be a good role modelparents should always be positive, calm, and confident in themselves. They should always encourage their children to strive for bigger and better and must be satisfied and embrace their success or failure equally.

Being a good role model it is responsibility of the parents to help their children to become the best version of themselves, help them to set a list of the key characteristics that they want to achieve , identify their negative aspects and helping them out in making the improvements.

They completely trust and rely on you and are actually visualizing what you are doing. So, beware of what you are doing and how you are behaving in front of them. Don't give them advice instead act. Suppose if your kid is watching a famous TV Serial, ChotaBheem all the day. Don't say to him that, "don't watch TV and you do it by yourself. Scolding them and getting or snatching the remote from him and turning your favorite channel will create a mindset that watching TV is not bad, instead of watching Chotabheem is the bad thing and they will stick to this imaginary concept.

Parents themselves should have a good relationship with all the family members and if not still they must try not to behave badly to the elderly people in front of the children because what you row in their minds today that you have to reap tomorrow. So, you should never ever give them a chance to do that.

Also, sometimes you might have some point to argue with your spouse, but never do it in front of the children. Just make them engage in other activities until your arguments are over and if possible just postpone the arguments to the night when the child sleeps.

Also, it is also important to inculcate yourself with good habits like getting up early in the morning, doing yoga, practicing exercise not for once in a while but consistently. If the child observes that you are practicing these habits on a daily basis they will automatically start practicing and will develop good habits which in turn is important in shaping up of their positive attitude and their future.

Doing yoga with Child

It is also important to get involved with any kind of fun activity with the family like Laughter Therapy, spending a fine Sunday evening together enjoying with your family etc. Doing this will help the child to get involved with family activities and sharing a beautiful bond with the family.

Last, but not least discuss your financial terms in front of the children. As per studies, the financial aspect of every child and the secret key to the treasure of the financial intelligence is learned from their parents only. So, ask them to handle cash even if it is in smaller amounts. And if you have some loans don't hesitate to discuss the same with your child. Let your child knows that and this is absolutely fine.

Once they understand your financial terms or if you make them understand your financial terms in a proper manner there is a probability for them to cut down their extravagant expenses. Don't create an imaginary financial condition of your own home. One day or other they will know the original situation and it might break down them psychologically and the results may be disastrous.

It is also noted that the parents are doing everything in a proper manner but still, the child is not following them. If this is the case with you as well you need not worry. Remember the proverb,

"Rome wasn't built in a day". So, it may take ome time. Have patience but the results will be worth it.

4.Let your children speak you listen

As parents, you really need to understand that the children have lots of ideas to explore and share it with someone. So, it is your responsibility to listen to them very patiently even if does not have any sense. Just give them a chance to speak with you.

School plays a Vital role :

Pampering routineafter school

When they are back from the school and you too have returned from the office just spent a quality time with them. You can sit with them without TV and mobile phonesfor a few minutes and allow them to speak. Encourage them to explain their day to day activities in school that might be about their class teachers, classmates, friends, fight with friends etc. So all you need here is to be consistent to this activity as it would be beneficial to both of you and you will be impressed after the results. When you really listen to them and their stories you can easily analyze by your instinct that whether they are telling a lie or whether they are in moving towards the right path. Also, your child spent most of the time in the school so you also need to visit the school at least once a month and have a conversation with their teachers in person.

Midst of conversation mode :

 Sometimes you might be in some discussion with your neighbors or relatives and I am not very sure whether this thing happens in the metro cities or not. To be precise in metro cities you might be on a telephonic conversation with your friends or siblings or video conferencing call with your some relatives. And at that time they might come near you, sit and listen to your conversation. In the midst of the conversation they always try to explain some point, but what we generally do is, we ignore them. Instead, you have to give them a moment, you need to pause and let them speak, because sometimes they may have some genuine points related to the conversation.

And that you are not raising your children for neighbors, relatives, or some other people. Therefore, allow them to speak even if it may be irrelevant because it really doesn't matter at all.

Never think that they don't know anything as you have not discussed such a topic with them before. Remember they are learning a lot from their school, surroundings, and society. Today's generation is smarter than us because they have more exposure from various sources.

And so if they speak you can easily understand their knowledge, their observing power etc. It is indeed an important step in the process of parenting. If you want to correct their mistakes, let them speak in a way they want.

5.Correcting Mistakes

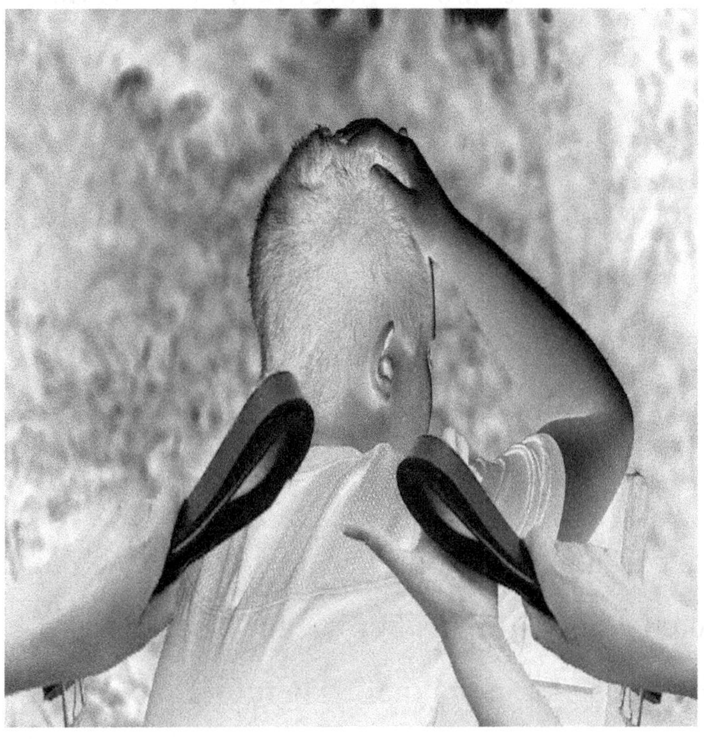

Correcting mistakes of the children are an important aspect of parenting. If you are too strict they may break down and if you are too lenient they may take everything as they want. So, it is your utmost responsibility to handle them properly.

The first step in correcting their mistakes is to identify them. You should never compromise on the mistakes of your child.

Let me narrate it with an example where your child gets 40 marks in English and his/her friend got 70 marks. In this situation, you need not make comparisons because firstly it is not a mistake and secondly it would create an inferiority complex within them that is not good for one's future.

Let me explain another scenario where your child has taken a pen from his/her friend. And, that is merely a mistake, not a theft. Therefore, you need to identify between the mistake and a theft. If you don't identify the difference between the two you will be unable to correct the mistakes of your children

After you identify their mistakes you have to make them understand as well and that is the most important thing that the child will not do the mistake again. If you don't make them understand you can't even correct them by scolding or beating. The Last step in the process of correcting mistakes after identifying is to make them realize their mistakes. It is an important step because without self-realization of the mistakes they are probably going to do the mistakes again.

As parents, you don't have to encourage your child when they do mistakes because they don't understand what they are doing and the difference between right and wrong. If they are doing good things express your appreciation and if they are doing mistakes you have correct them without any compromise.

6.MORALS/ VALUES/TRADITIONS

Moral values play an important role in shaping up of your child's character. As a parent you have to imbibe the moral values and Indian traditions to your children during the early stages of his growth.Moral values are what motivates our behavior and ground our judgments about what is good or bad, desirable or undesirable. Some examples of moral values are: honesty, forgiveness, telling the truth, being courageous, keeping promises,do not gossip, treating others as you want to be treated.

Nowadays with the rising demand for electronic gadgets and internet, you child is learning something or the other every day. So under this influence, they don't understand morals values, ethics, and rich Indian traditions. Therefore, you need to educate the morals values and traditions at the right time to your child otherwise they will set a different meaning for everything which might not suit your family values.

Let me explain this with an example; suppose your child wants to wear a modern dress for a pilgrimage visit. Make them understand that is not our culture or tradition. By saying so, I am not against wearing a modern dress because nowadays we need to check for the comfort factor of the children in wearing a dress rather than looking for traditions. But the thing is, whatever your caste is, the Indian values and traditions will not allow anyone to wear ultra-modern dress to any religious places as a mark of respect to such places. Make them understand that you can wear a party dress to a party, not to a pilgrimage.

Make them understand that we are a heritage rich country with morals values, ethics and cultures right fromspirituality, holy books, prayer methods, dressing style, food habits, long- term relationship maintenance and so on.

Don't Forget our Roots:

You may live in a metro city, getting remuneration in lakhs, have an individual villa with a posh car but do remember your roots. You might be from some village don't get annoyed because 80% of the India is villages only. Now you may have a different lifestyle from your parents. But, try to imbibe the roots to your children. If you can go Bali for a summer vacation, it means you can easily visit once in a year to your hometown where you originally belong to. Don't hesitate to discuss the roots with your child because if they don't know their roots they will be unable to know what their culture is all about.

HOW WE HAVE TO INCULCATE MORAL VALUES & TRADITIONS IN OUR CHILDREN:

We are a heritage rich country with rich values, ethics and cultures. It is the prime responsibility of the parents to educate the children of our values and culture because culture develops and grows up through an accumulation of actions, traditions, ceremonies, and rituals that are closely aligned with that vision and that too nothing happens overnight.

Below are some Moral Values & Tradition how we need to Inculcate in our children:

Importance of Family Life: We just need to teach our children the importance of family values in our lives and how it acts as a support system we can truly rely upon at all times and in all situations. Therefore, this is the most important factor responsible for inculcating moral and ethical values in children.

Respect for elders: Respecting our elders is the most valuable tradition in our country that is prevalent since ages. And we need to imbibe this value to our children so that they will continue to uphold this tradition for elders, enforce a sense of order and discipline in families.

Celebrating Festivals: It is the need of the hour to educate the children about what Indian culture and festivals are all about. We need to educate them about the scientific meanings and significant values behind each and every festival.

Furthermore, it is the responsibility of the parents to know and to make the children understand that Indian culture has been intertwined with scientific reasons and is not superstitious. The present day children are not interested to know about Indian culture because they feel Indian culture to be full of superstitious beliefs.

Few points how to make children aware of Indian Traditions & Culture:

- Give Example of Indian culture.
- Follow Indian culture.
- Watch Indian cultural programs.
- Tell Indian cultural Stories.
- Talk to them about diverse Indian culture.
- Make trips to different regions of India.
- Teach Indian values.
- Encourage traditional dressing and food.
- Teach them to respect Indian culture.

Carry on your Traditions

Indian Culture is distinctive and it is one of the oldest cultures of the world. Every aspect of Indian Culture is unique in its way. It is truly the responsibility of parents to make the children aware of rich Indian culture at an early age. Children should follow and respect Indian culture.

Morals values and traditions together form an important aspect in shaping up your child's personality. Now with the increasing use of the internet and social media and that electronic gadgets are easily available, there are rare chances that your child will understand and respect morals values and our age -old traditions.

Children today are torn between our Indian traditions and the Western culture or modernity. Today we live in a multicultural society, which is a byproduct of globalization. Therefore, teaching children about Indian traditions and culture and the environment we live in is of utmost importance.

Practice what you preach :

 Teaching the morals values only is not sufficient until and unless you follow them. If you follow the rules firstly by yourself then they will follow it or else they don't. If you want your child to be healthy, you have to give them a wholesome nutrition. So you insist them to eat fruits and vegetables on a daily basis that they just ignore.

Let me explain the scenario in a clear way. Like every parent, you also want your child to be healthy and so you include fruits and vegetables in their diet. But, you must include, first in your diet because they observe you all the times. They observe your daily day to day activities if whatever you are eating is really healthy. So always practice what you preach to them.

<u>**Carry on with explanations :**</u>

If you want your child to follow a particular tradition just explain them with good reasons. Suppose if you don't know the reason for a particular tradition simply accept your ignorance and try to find out the reason for that particular tradition. This step is very important in designing the character of the new generation.

And the conclusion we need to handle morals values and traditions with the utmost care and pass on to the next generation.

Gadget Addiction

Electronic gadgets are increasingly becoming an inseparable part of the lives of our children. Child gadget addiction is becoming worse day by day and as the years goes by. Children nowadays spend most of their time on electronic gadgets like their smartphones, the TV, the computer, etc. and are no longer are interested to go out and play.

And this gadget addiction is deteriorating the lives and habits of the children. So as a parent you must look out for signs of technology addiction in your child and if you find that your child is turning into a gadget addict it is the high time for you to step in and curb their habits.

Some parents feel that electronic gadgets are like stress busters for the children. The thing is when your child is back from the school he needs some sort of relaxation and so he watches TV, uses a smartphone. In other words, he is more into electronic gadgets that have games, cartoons, his favorite TV serials etc. But have you ever thought of your own exposure to electronic gadgets when you were a kid? You have been waiting for a whole week to watch your favorite show that too with a lot of constraints from your parents. Nowadays everything is open. You kid can see any show anytime and anywhere. Of course, it is the outcome of technology but it may spoil your child both physically and psychologically. However, at the same time, I must admit that I am not against technology instead we have to use technology in a right manner at the right time for our child.

After school pampering routine:

The new generation is actually staying away from the physical activity after returning from school. Just remember they are sitting in the same place for 8 hours a day and so they must be involved in some sort of physical activity like playing volleyball, playing cricket, outdoor games etc. And most of the children stick straight to the TV after returning from school wills only leads to health hazards. Most of the parents easily allow children to watch TV after school so that they can do their work very easily without any disturbances. So, it clearly indicates that you don't want to engage with them and so you are easily allowing them to watch TV.

Therefore, if you allow this habit to continue, the children will not engage with the people around themselves and maybe not even with you. This would leave to an imaginary world among themselves which would eventually lead to relationship malfunction.

<u>Give Them healthy Indian Snacks :</u>

There are so many Indian snacks which are available at very affordable prices. So, there is no need to feed junk foods, sugar-laden items etc. to your child which leads to an unhealthy lifestyle. Make them understand our rich food habits along with the super values of Indian Spices,

Use Technology – Use Smart Class rooms Oriented Schools :

Let your children be aware of the things that happen around them. In the home we have to look after them very carefully for the usage of the mobile internet because most of our connections are not disconnected from the unwanted sites or YouTube channels. In contrary to this schools are very efficient in teaching the technology to the students in a positive and constructive way. They make the students understand that technology is not only about social media channels like Facebook, Instagram, YouTube and other entertainment but technology has a broader meaning   and so if used wisely it can really help us in changing our lives.

Also, you should never blame your children for using unwanted technology for example recently a famous unwanted game "BLUE WHALE was launched which proved disastrous and ended up in killings of a number of students in different parts of the country. So, all you need to make them understand and realize the disastrous effects of technology are not used in a right way.

Best After school routine :

Engage your child in some routine work when he is back from school. The best routine after school is to make your children play either inside or outside. Let their clothes get dirty and mind fresh. This is the holistic development you need to incorporate in our child.

Allow them to speak and fight with others of their age groups which in turn are theways better than to being isolated or involved with gadgets.

Gadget Addiction

Let them Make some Mistakes

Let you allow your children to make some mistakes and don't expect them to be perfect in all aspects. You can, of course, scold your children once in a while but try not to make it a regular routine. You are the parents, the creators of your children if they are afraid of you they will start hiding from you. And now, if they commit a mistake you are unaware of and you will come to you by someone else even at that time you will be only one to solve their problem.

Therefore, it is your duty not to make them afraid of you. Encourage them to speak truth to you for whatever the things. Make them feel easy and confortable when they want to share something with you.

Let me explain this with a simple scenario; suppose they have broken a car mirror. Don't scold them at once. Firstly, discuss the problem by giving them an opportunity to speak about what exactly happened because sometimes it would really not their mistake. It may be the mistake of the other boy who played with your child and has run away. And when your child touches the mirror it may fell down. In this situation, you need to handle the situation with patience.

Now even if it has been done by your kid just makes them understand that it is his own car and it is his money. If you spend money on repairing the car mirror you cannot give him pocket money. The key is to make him understand very smartly and try to make him realize that money should be valued at all times. So try to understand him of the mistakes so that he will not repeat it again.

In contrary, now If you will handle this situation by beating him and scolding him severely and saying "Hey it's my money; you don't understand how hard I have been working to earn this money?" Doing this, children would never ever understand or realize their mistakes and will never be open to you.

And secondly, at present, you are superior to them and so they will listen to you. But when they grow up and turn into mature and responsible ones at that time when you try to say something to with them they will say "Will you please shut up and mind your own business "

So, the conclusion is you need to be a friendly parent and it is quite normal if a child is making mistakes.

Give them an opportunity as we get an opportunity from our senior manager for not doing a presentation properly. Make your child understand the way we understood and they will understand for sure because at the end they are also human beings; provided if you explain them in a proper manner. If still, they don't understand your explanation you need to change your way of approach. So give them an opportunity to speak truth with you and embrace their mistakes and correct them very smartly.

Play date with children

Play Date

Do you believe play date with your children is the biggest gift that you can give them? The answer is yes, definitely. Let's get started with what the exact meaning of a play date is. Play date or play date is an expression primarily used in the US for an arranged appointment for children to get together for a few hours to play. **Play date** provides a fun and exciting environment where children can enjoy the play, listen to a variety of music, socialize, and meet people.

And self-initiated *play* improves a number of child skills such as guessing, figuring and interpreting which in turn is very important for the mental development of the children. Play date helps to improve concentration, focusing power, critical thinking in a better way.

Engage your children in some fun activities, playing with them make them happy and closer to you. Also physiologically it is proven that these activities will eventually help you to get out of your stress.

Nowadays, in our fast-paced lives we all have a lack of time and other factors. Just stop all these factors. Do this activity; fix up a monthly schedule for the play date and you will also feel refreshed. Instead of having a lazy Sunday on your couch with TV and snacks, you can try these activities at least once a month.

Here, what matters the most is the consistency. Having a play date with your child once a year during holidays is not beneficial in any of the ways. If you cannot afford to organize play dates, just go to the beach and play volleyball with them. Or you can simply visit the nearby park and play football with your child. The thing is you have numerous opportunities if you are really willing to do it.

Indulging in these activities will be like stress busters for both parents and the children. Furthermore, the children will learn teamwork, team spirit, and self-discipline all the habits that will help to shape the child's future in an organized way.

How to set the Perfect Play date for your children:

Below are some ways to get the perfect play date

1. **Prepare in advance is the Key: It** is very important to plan in advance for the play date. Also, you have to make sure your child is relaxed, involved and not hungry at all.

    2. Set a Definite Start and End Time for Your Playdate: It becomes easier when you start and end the play date with a definite start and end time.

3. Limit the number of Kids:

It is recommended to start with 4-5 families at the start of the first play date. Because you won't feel much pressure to attend so many people at the same time and your event will also be cozier. And in doing so, everyone will get the chance to get to know each other very well.

4. Prepare Your Child to Host:

 It will be the best practice to serve your child as the host at the playmate. So, it is your responsibility to prepare them and make them understand what's going to happen. Also, you need to mentally prepare your child as other kids will be playing with his toys, tearing the home, throwing cushions, getting everything out of the place so that he will be more comfortable with the different activities of other kids.

Lock up Your Pets behind the bars: It is advisable to lock the pets on the play date as a courtesy to your guests and other kids. Because some kids develop allergies when they pull the tail of pets or play with them.

Plan One Structured Activity:

It will always be the best thing if you plan some kind of **structured activity** to get the kids to settle down right before they leave.Free play is good to go with; followed by motivating them to create their own picture frames, painting or get involved with some kind of family crafts.

Have Fun!

In the end, a play date should be full of fun both for the kids and the parents. Remember you're hosting for just an hour or two and gives you some time to refresh and connect with other moms who are going through the same with every passing day. So, when you will plan your play date the next time, just relax, sit back and enjoy every moment of it.

<u>Never leave them alone:</u>

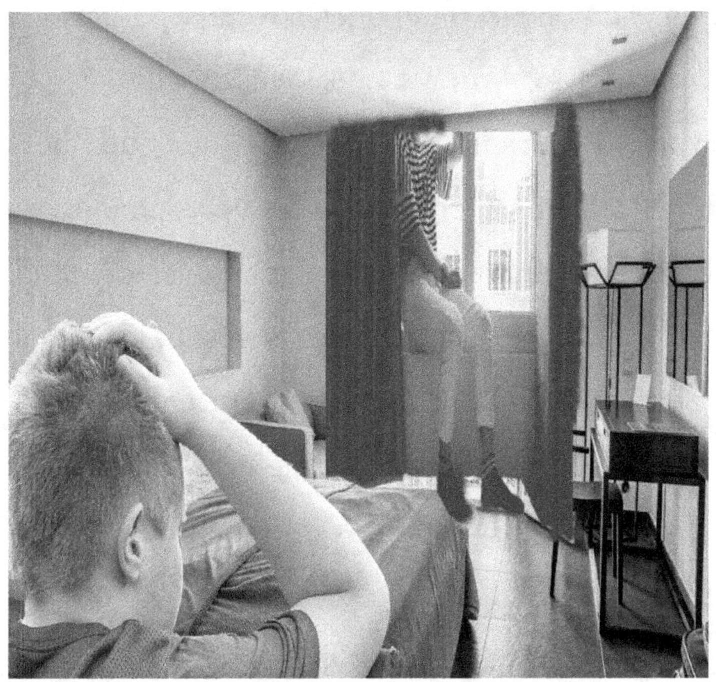

During our childhood, we all have a common hall where all the family members used to sit together, eat, fight and enjoy together. We almost do all the works in a commonplace; we all share a common TV but nowadays we have inherited a different culture from the West that everybody should have a separate room and now even the siblings of the same blood are not interested to share the same room. To be clear, if we have two children each one of them does have a separate room and that's our new status symbol which is disastrous to your children. Because the bond, the attachment, the brother-sisterhood Do you believe play date with your children is the biggest gift that you can give them? The answer is yes, definitely. Engage your children into fun activities, playing with them make them happy and closer to you. Also physiologically it is proven that these activities will eventually help you to get out of your stress.

We all know that children can learn any good or bad things but as a parent, it is your duty to always make them travel in the right direction. Don't think that you are parents and that you should not indulge in their activities. That's absolutely wrong. Just live the life with them and you will feel more refreshed, motivated, disciplined and will enjoy your life.

When parents are present in the home it is often noticed that the child sits in her/his room. As parents, we really do not have an idea of what exactly she/ he are doing in the room. We can just make our assumptions that the child might be doing this and that because we believe we cannot monitor their activities every single moment and so we let it happen.

So, when you are at home never let them go out of your sight; please don't allow them to get a separate room until of certain age when it is really required. This activity will help to design the character of the child and get rid of unwanted things.

When your child develops a habit of being alone and sitting in a separate room they can develop very easily develop bad habits and will not be physiologically fit to face the day to day situations. If you are not interacting and guiding them in a proper manner then unnecessary relationships at such small ages may affect them easily because after all man in a social animal. They never wanted isolation but need someone to express their feelings whether it is happiness, sorrow, weird or anything else. If you will not allow them to express it with you then they will search for some other person. You should not be proud to say that my child is calm and composed sitting in his/her room. Instead, look for the reasons why he always tries to find a separate space.

Remind yourself of the days when you used to study or prepare for the board exams and your parents used to cut the TV or cable connection until you finish the exams. You also do the study in a commonplace.

So the procedure, the concept needs to be given a deep thought? Can't we practice the same old procedure to our children that we have inherited from our parents?

Dinner Together

Dinner with Family

A dining table is a perfect place to get together with your family and so should truly be a family time. And it is very important to stay connected with your family for a healthy relationship. We all go for work, run behind money and no one has time for each other. But you can manage to have just 20 minutes for your dinner with your children and spouse with no electronic devices, phones etc. Therefore, the need of the hour is to give some quality time dedicatedly to your children so that they can express their views and thoughts to you. As a parent, you always have to be their best friends with an eagle eye and it your duty to guide the child in the right way.

Giving your children the freedom is the most important key to make them fly in their world. Spent quality time with them. Just discuss the whole day experience some days it may be good while some days may be bad. Nevertheless, the mood participates in this activity which would really refresh your mood and makes you mind calm. Listening and entering visually into their world is the most important aspect of parenting. And that's actually an incredible experience too. So enjoy it! If you started enjoying it, you will never miss this event.

Do this activity almost on all the days. However, if not possible due to your hectic schedule just fix a few specific days as per your schedule and gradually you will see the bond getting closer between you, your child and your spouse

Growing up with children!

Parenting is an art. Parenting does not mean that you are growing up your children; instead, you have to grow with them. During childhood of your child, you have to correct his path if he is leading a wrong one. When the children reach adulthood phase or teenage phase what we as a parent usually do is we try to implement the strict criteria's to correct them which doesn't work at all because at that particular stage they actually have their own point of view.

Guiding and setting their path in a good direction should be the ultimate goal of every parent. When your child grows older just put your hands on his shoulder be with them with updated knowledge and never be shy to accept your ignorance.

If you are leading them towards the right path and they are not accepting just leave them for with their own ideas for that particular moment. Sooner or later they will understand that their path is wrong and at that time they will come to you. At that moment, act immediately. Don't blame them or ignore them. You need to cuddle them and solve the problem in a way so that they will never ever repeat the same mistake again in life.

Children keep themselves updated with new technologies and techniques and have very good exposure to the outer world. And therefore they think whatever they are doing is correct but they really don't understand that you have a valuable thing than the new technologies and that's the "Experience" which they cannot buy anywhere. So, travel with them with their new technologies and your experience which in turn is the true parenting.

Join the hands of the children, give them freedom and fly in the sky of their world make them corrected till the end of your life. LET's CELEBRATE IT!!

Final Thoughts:

Bedtime stories:

Bedtime stories with moral values plays an important role in developing better psychology inculcate good values to the kids. Getting better sleep gives good refreshing thoughts in their dream probably, where the values of the children can be enriched much better. As a Parent spend just 15 minutes for this Activity.

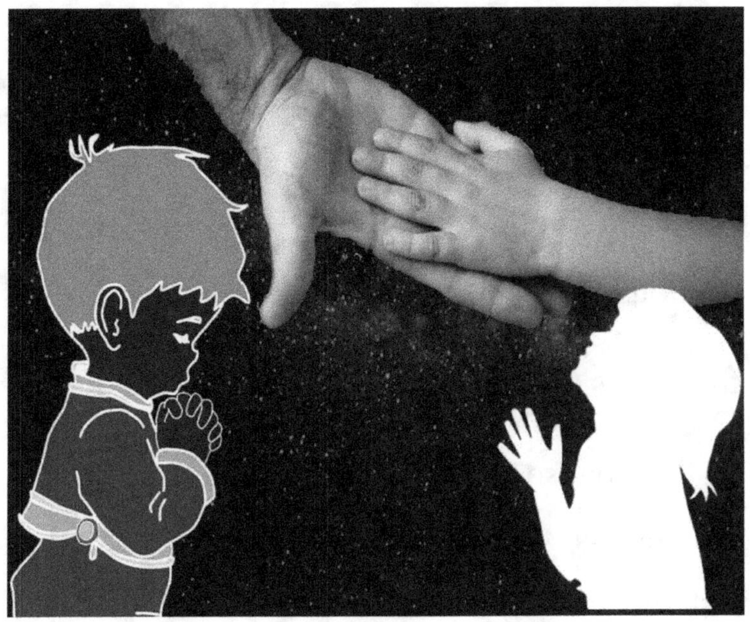

It is our parental duty to feed them good values because what you sow is what you reap; Practice gratitude with them, then asks them to do gratitude prayer and this prayer really helps those to avid of bad habits or characters like jealousy etc.

Sample Gratitude for Children (Practice)

1. Thank you god for giving me the day

2. Thank you god for giving me my parents

3. Thank you god for giving me good food

4. Thank you god for giving me good dress

5. Thank you god for giving me beautiful house

Both Parents Cooperation:

If suppose child has done a mistake, and if one parent is scolding for the mistake the other parent should not be in favor of the child because child is very small in age and they don't realize the mistake until both the parents say the same Point, so be careful in this point while handling and molding up the children.

"The complete book provide a list of activities in which both parents and child has to be involved, if it is been practiced in a consistent manner you will get proven results" laimer:

*blue whale game is been requested to ban in India, because it creates several suicide cases in India

*Indian values are not against wearing modern dresses but wearing jeans in some temples is banned in India.

* The points of the author does not hurt any religion or any person but insist their own point of view.

* There may be some images which was downloaded from Google and it is free to use, if there is any copyright intended please inform us.

Author bio:

Nancy Samuel has formal educational in clinical psychology, as a parent does parental counseling to various parents with parental problems. Parental education is necessary for young parents who are really working on a very hectic schedule, have this book as your reference and practice this activity consistently to yield good results.

Nancy Samuel an assistant of Dr.V.Geeta , MBBS DPM., Psycatrist who is having more than 29+ years of experience. This book has valid activities and exercises that have been presented to you. We have done various surveys to the parents and what has worked for the parents that technique only discussed here. All the activities here, when they are performed with consistency yield unexpected results from your child in a positive manner.

Review Request:

Please provide your honest review after reading this book in Amazon, it would be helpful for us to grow better. Also provide your email to us. send your valuable thoughts, if you want to subscribe to the newsletter please send a mail to the above mail id! Thanks for your support!